ILLUMINATION STATION™ DEVOTIONAL

SHINING A LIGHT ON JESUS

Written by Rhonda VanCleave

INTRODUCTION

Who *is* Jesus? If you ask this question to people you know, you may get different answers. One day, Jesus even asked His disciples who people said He was. The Bible shows us clearly that it doesn't matter what others think—Jesus is who God and His Word (the Bible) say He is. These thirty devotions give you a chance to shine a light on who Jesus is and what being His disciple (follower) means.

A devotional is a great way to have a quiet time with God and allow the Holy Spirit to help you know more about Jesus. In this book, the theme of illumination and light guides that time of learning. Each devotion has four main parts:

1. The **SPOTLIGHT DEVOTION** will give you a Bible verse or two to focus on, followed by a short message to think about from Scripture.
2. **SEARCHLIGHT VERSES** is a challenge activity that suggests a way you can dig into God's Word with related Scriptures for that day.
3. The **BRIGHT IDEA** feature contains either a fun fact about light and light-related things or an activity based on the fun facts you've learned.
4. Finally, **REFLECTIONS** is your space to think and process. You can journal or doodle your thoughts about what you've learned. You can write prayers or questions to God. A suggestion is given for each day, but use that space to do whatever you like!

Enjoy this time learning about God who created light, Jesus who *is* the Light of the world, and all the wonderful ways we can reflect the love and light of Jesus to those around us.

ISBN: 979-8-3845-4592-7

Dewey Decimal Classification: C242.62
Subject Heading: DEVOTIONAL LITERATURE \ JESUS CHRIST \ HOPE
Printed in the United States of America
1 2 3 4 5 6 • 29 28 27 26

CONTENTS

JESUS IS GOD'S PROMISED SON

JESUS IS GOD'S PERFECT SON

JESUS IS THE POWERFUL SON OF GOD

JESUS IS THE PROVEN SON OF GOD

JESUS IS GOD'S PLAN FOR FORGIVENESS

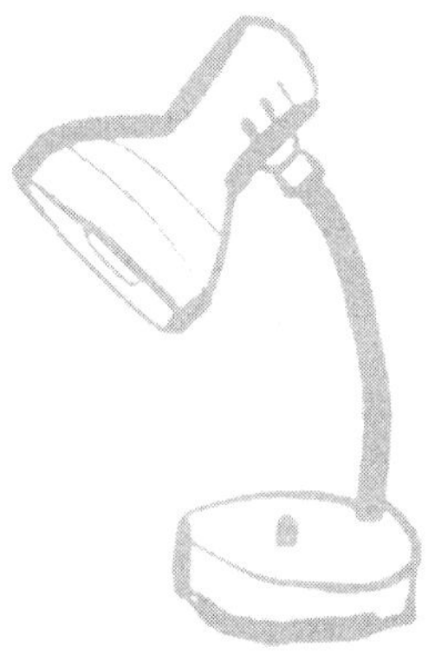

The Source of All Light

Then God said, "Let there be light," and there was light.—Genesis 1:3

Have you ever thought about the importance of light? Time as we know it began when God created the heavens and the earth, including light, land, water, plants, trees, fish, birds, animals, and humans. All of it was designed by God. He made everything perfectly and in a logical order, starting with *light*. Everything that followed needed light to see, grow, and function.

Light is why we see color and often how we feel warmth. It helps living things grow and can even affect our mood. After God created light, Genesis 1:4 says, "God saw that the light was good." God called the light "day" and the darkness "night." That was the first day.

In this devotional we will discover that God is not only the source of light, He *is* light! Scripture tells us Jesus is the Light of the world. He was there in the beginning when all things were created (John 1:1–3), and He came to earth to help us know about God and His love for us. He came so we can understand that disobeying God is sin and why sin breaks our relationship with God. Because Jesus took our punishment, we can have forgiveness of sins and a promise of eternal life. Each of these devotions will shine a light on Jesus and help you learn even more about who He really is!

Pray

Ask God to help you learn more about Jesus, the Light of the world.

Searchlight Verses

Read John 1:1–3 aloud. Then read it again and say "Jesus" instead of "the Word." How does that help you understand those verses?

BRIGHT IDEA: SUNS AND STARS

The brightest light we can see is the sun. Our sun is a star, the only one in our solar system. The stars you see in the sky that twinkle are "suns" that are far, far away. (Planets don't twinkle.) Our sun is bigger than some stars, but astronomers have also found some stars that are one hundred times bigger than our sun!

REFLECTIONS

Write about the darkest place you've ever been. How did you feel when you finally had some light?

A Light for the Nations

"I will appoint you to be a covenant for the people and a light to the nations."—Isaiah 42:6

Have you ever walked at night with a small flashlight and wished you had a brighter light because it was way too dark outside? No darkness is too much for God's light; the Bible tells us He is a light to the nations!

God created a perfect world, but people disobeyed Him. That is sin, and it broke the relationship between God and people. He established a covenant (or promise) with people, telling them what to do as their part of the covenant. God's part was a plan to restore the relationship sin had broken. The people tried to keep their part of the covenant, but they slowly drifted back into disobeying God. Over and over again, God would forgive the people's sins, and things would get better, but then the people would disobey Him again.

But God kept His promise. He sent His Son, Jesus, to restore the relationship sin had broken. Jesus did things no one before or since has been able to do. He obeyed God completely, and He was a light in the darkness to all people of all nations.

Pray

Thank God for keeping His promise and sending His Son, Jesus.

Searchlight Verses

After Jesus was born, His earthly parents took Him to the temple "to present Him to the Lord." This was a Jewish law. Every firstborn male child was to be presented at the temple. Read what happened when Mary and Joseph brought Jesus to the temple in Luke 2:25–32 (especially verse 32).

Bright Idea: Make a Suncatcher

You'll need a paper plate, scissors, clear contact paper or clear packing tape, various colors of tissue paper, a hole punch, and yarn.

Cut out the center of the paper plate. Cover the opening with clear contact paper or overlapping rows of clear packing tape. Carefully place the plate on the table with the sticky side up. Cut small squares of tissue paper. Arrange them any way you like to completely cover the sticky circle. Punch a hole along the top edge of the paper plate. String a length of yarn through the hole and knot the two ends together to make a loop. Hang the suncatcher in a light-filled window to enjoy the shining colors.

Reflections

What are your favorite things to do on a sunny day? How does the sun's light make you feel? Write about it below or draw a picture of the sunny-day things you enjoy.

The Promised Light

The people walking in darkness have seen a great light; a light has dawned on those living in the land of darkness.—Isaiah 9:2

Prophets were people chosen by God to share His messages. Many of them—including Isaiah, Micah, Hosea, Zechariah, and even King David—wrote about what would happen when God's Promised Messiah came to earth. Isaiah described the Jewish people as walking in darkness. But one day they would see "a great light"—Jesus!

More than seventy Old Testament prophecies are about the coming Messiah. The New Testament writers knew the Scriptures and often quoted these Old Testament prophecies in the books and letters they wrote. But before Jesus was born, there was a period of about four hundred years when no new prophecies were given. None! The people waited and waited for the prophecies to be fulfilled. And they were! In God's perfect timing, He fulfilled the prophecies about the Promised Messiah.

How could so many tiny details, shared hundreds of years before, come true? They came true because God was and is in control. What He promised about Jesus happened! As Isaiah had prophesied, a Light had now dawned.

Pray

Talk to God about how amazing He truly is.

Searchlight Verses

Read these Scriptures to discover some other prophecies and fulfillments about Jesus:

	Prophecy	**Fulfillment**
Born in Bethlehem	Micah 5:2	Luke 2:4–7
Called out of Egypt	Hosea 11:1	Matthew 2:13–15
Descendant of King David	1 Chronicles 17:11–15	Matthew 1:1
Crucified	Psalm 22:16	John 19:18

Bright Idea: Changing Shadows

A shadow forms when something blocks a source of light. Your shadow might change direction or size when you are outside on a sunny day. That's because, as the earth rotates, the sun's position changes. Try standing outside in the mid-morning and ask someone to trace your shadow with chalk. Stand in the same place in mid-afternoon and ask a friend to trace your shadow again. How did your shadow change?

Reflections

What are some things around you that change? What things about God never change?

PREPARING THE WAY

For he is the one spoken of through the prophet Isaiah, who said: A voice of one crying out in the wilderness: Prepare the way for the Lord; make his paths straight!—Matthew 3:3

God planned the arrival of Jesus the Messiah perfectly. Long before Jesus was born, God's prophets wrote about someone who would announce that the Messiah's time had come. Luke 1:5–25 tells the amazing story of a priest named Zechariah and his wife, Elizabeth, who were too old to have a baby. One day, an angel of the Lord told Zechariah some shocking news: the couple would have a son, and they were to name the baby John.

When John was born, Zechariah prophesied, "And you, child, will be called a prophet of the Most High, for you will go before the Lord to prepare his ways" (Luke 1:76). This child, John, would one day prepare the world for the coming Messiah! When John grew up, he told people about Jesus. He was called John the Baptist because he baptized those who wanted to show they had repented of their sins. (You can read about it in Matthew 3:1–6.) John preached in the wilderness, ate locusts and wild honey, and was known for wearing a camel-hair garment and leather belt.

People came from all around to hear what this odd-looking man had to say. They might have been curious when they heard about John, but his preaching pointed them to Jesus and made them realize they were sinners against God. Many confessed their sins, and John baptized them in the Jordan River.

PRAY

Thank God for the first people who told you about Jesus.

SEARCHLIGHT VERSES

Read the prophecies in the Scriptures below. What do they say about John the Baptist?

Isaiah 40:3–5 Malachi 3:1

BRIGHT IDEA: SHADOW TRACING

Place a piece of drawing paper on the ground or a table. Stand a toy animal or another small solid object on the edge of the paper. Place a light source (lamp, flashlight, or the sun if outside) so that the object's shadow is on the paper. Trace around the shadow. Does the shadow's size change if you move the light source closer or farther away?

REFLECTIONS

A shadow lets you know something is there. John let people know Jesus was coming. Make a list of people who helped you know about Jesus, or draw pictures of places where you have learned about Jesus.

GOD'S ANOINTED ONE

He began by saying to them, "Today as you listen, this Scripture has been fulfilled."—Luke 4:21

Jesus was born and grew up like all people do. This was something God had promised through the prophets. When Jesus was about thirty years old and had officially begun His ministry, He returned to the synagogue in the town of Nazareth, where He had spent most of His younger years. There, Jesus read from the Isaiah scroll. (Scripture wasn't in books then; it was hand-copied onto scrolls. You can read the same words in Isaiah 61:1–2.) The words said that "the Spirit of the Lord God is on me, because the Lord has anointed me to bring good news to the poor." When Jesus finished reading, He said, "Today as you listen, this Scripture has been fulfilled."

Wow—the prophecy had been fulfilled! God's Anointed One had come! Wouldn't you think people would be excited about the good news? At first the people in Jesus's hometown were amazed by His words, but then they became angry. They thought God's Anointed One would come to save the Jewish people, but Jesus was saying He had come for everyone, not just the Jews! Rather than being happy, the people of Nazareth drove Jesus out of town.

This story is a reminder that Jesus faced challenges just like we do. He knows how hard it can be to share God's truth with family and friends.

PRAY

Ask God to give you courage when you have an opportunity to talk to your family about Jesus.

SEARCHLIGHT VERSES

Read Luke 4:16–30. What are some amazing parts of this story?

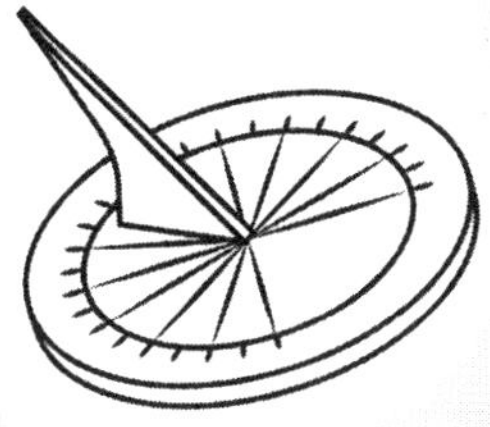

BRIGHT IDEA: SUNDIALS

Did you know shadows can help tell time? Sundials were some of the earliest clocks. They used the position of shadows to tell what time of day it was.

REFLECTIONS

Draw a simple picture of a person or an object such as a tree or a dog. Then try drawing its shadow. Think about where the light might be coming from to know where to position the shadow.

THE PROMISED MESSIAH

"You are the Messiah, the Son of the living God."—Matthew 16:16

During Jesus's time, the Jewish people knew God had promised a Messiah—a Savior. The Roman empire was in power, and many Jews believed if the Messiah came, He would be their earthly king. He would get rid of the Roman government. But God's plan was much bigger than overthrowing the people's current rulers. God's plan was to provide a Savior with eternal power.

Jesus was not what the people were expecting. Even when He performed miracles and taught with authority, they still did not understand that He was God's Promised Messiah.

One day Jesus asked His chosen disciples, "Who do people say I am?" Some of the answers were "John the Baptist," "Elijah," "Jeremiah," or another one of the prophets who had died and come back. Then Jesus asked, "But you, who do you say that I am?" Peter spoke up. "You are the Messiah, the Son of the living God."

Peter was right! Jesus said Peter could only know this truth because God the Father had revealed it to him. Just like with Peter, God helps us know that Jesus is His Promised Son who came to be our Savior.

PRAY

God shows us who Jesus really is. Ask God to help you know and understand more about Jesus, the Promised Messiah and Savior of the world.

SEARCHLIGHT VERSES

You can read the whole conversation between Jesus and His disciples in Matthew 16:13–20. Look carefully at verse 20. Why do you think Jesus told the disciples not to tell anyone He was the Messiah?

BRIGHT IDEA: SHADOW PUPPETS

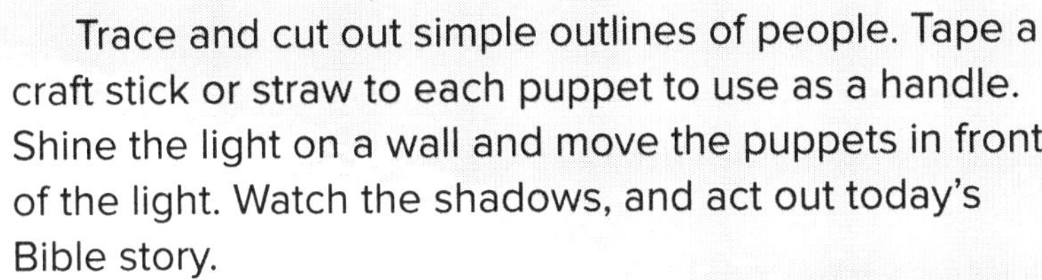

You'll need heavy paper (poster board or construction paper), scissors, craft sticks or straws, tape, and a light source (like a flashlight or any light that can be directed at the wall).

Trace and cut out simple outlines of people. Tape a craft stick or straw to each puppet to use as a handle. Shine the light on a wall and move the puppets in front of the light. Watch the shadows, and act out today's Bible story.

REFLECTIONS

You are learning more about Jesus all the time. Make a list of things you already know about Him.

Baptized and Beloved

A voice came from heaven: "You are my beloved Son; with you I am well-pleased."—Mark 1:11

How do we know Jesus is God's Son? Anyone can claim to be someone important, but where's the proof that helps us know who Jesus is? God provided proof in so many ways. We have already read about how Jesus fulfilled prophecies given hundreds of years earlier. God the Father helped Peter know Jesus was the Messiah. And when Jesus was baptized, God used a voice to let it be known that Jesus was His Son!

Jesus went to the Jordan River to be baptized by John the Baptist. At first John refused because he did not feel worthy to baptize the Son of God. After all, Jesus never sinned, and He always obeyed God the Father.

But God's plan was for Jesus to be baptized, so John agreed. As soon as Jesus came up out of the water, the heavens opened. God's Spirit came down like a dove, and a voice could be heard from heaven saying, "You are my beloved Son; with you I am well-pleased." Can you imagine seeing the dove come down and hearing a voice from heaven? What better proof could there be of who Jesus was and is?

Pray

Thank God for proving Jesus is truly His Son.

Searchlight Verses

Read John 1:6–9. Who was not the Light? Who is the true Light?

BRIGHT IDEA: EYE SEE!

How do eyes work? When light enters the eye, it is focused by the lens then converted into electrical signals by the retina. The signal travels on the optic nerve to the brain. The brain takes the signals and interprets them as the images that you see!

REFLECTIONS

Draw or make a list of things you can see right now. How many colors do you see?

The Light of the World

Jesus spoke to them again: "I am the light of the world. Anyone who follows me will never walk in the darkness but will have the light of life."—John 8:12

In the Bible, darkness often represents sin and a lack of understanding. Light represents righteousness and understanding. While Jesus was on earth, He was fully God *and* fully human. Only Jesus could brighten our darkness and help us understand who God is. As the Light of the world, Jesus provided a way to restore our relationship with God, a relationship broken by sin. Jesus showed us how to follow Him and ultimately how to live in the light with Him forever.

Sadly, some of the people who had the hardest time stepping out of the darkness and believing Jesus were the temple leaders. They were so sure of their own knowledge and so impressed with their own power that many of them failed to recognize the Messiah when He was standing there talking with them. Their confidence in their own goodness caused them to miss out on the truth that Jesus is the Light of the world.

We must remember we can't be good or righteous on our own. Trusting in Jesus begins with asking for forgiveness of our sins and continues with following Him as Savior and Lord.

Pray

Ask God to help you "see" and understand more about Jesus, the Light of the World.

Searchlight Verses

Some people rejected Jesus (and still do today) because they don't want to give up things they enjoy that are wrong according to God's Word. What does John 3:19–21 have to say about this?

BRIGHT IDEA: GET THE PICTURE

Challenge your family to see who can find the most sources of light in your house. Set a timer and start the search! When your time is up, compare notes. Who found the most items? Who found light sources no one else did? Talk about how much or how little light each item gives. Which lights do you want to turn on when you need to see clearly?

REFLECTIONS

Some people could not "clearly see" what Jesus was telling them even when He was right in front of them. Write about why you think people today have a hard time understanding who Jesus is.

Light Overcomes Darkness

In him was life, and that life was the light of men. That light shines in the darkness, and yet the darkness did not overcome it.—John 1:4–5

Have you ever noticed that no matter how dark a room is, the instant a light comes on, the darkness is gone? Light overcomes dark, not the other way around. Wherever the light reaches, things are more clearly seen.

When Jesus came to live on earth, He helped a lot of people see things about God that they didn't know or had misunderstood. Some people expected Jesus to immediately fix all the broken things in the world, but God is not a magic wand or a genie. Jesus performed many miracles, but He didn't stop all diseases or crime or other scary things. Until Jesus comes again, our world will still be "broken." However, His light has helped us see who God is and how much He cares for us. We can know that when God allows bad things to happen, He is still with us.

When we turn on a light in a dark room, the room doesn't change, but we do. We can see the truth of what's around us and feel more secure. Similarly, when we let Jesus's light shine into the dark areas of our lives, we see our circumstances differently and know that we are loved through them all.

Pray

Pray that your relationship with Jesus will grow more each day as you read your Bible, pray, and think about what God is teaching you.

Searchlight Verses

Read these three verses about the Lord being our light. Put a star by one you'd like to memorize:

Job 12:22
Psalm 18:28
Psalm 36:9

BRIGHT IDEA: EYEGLASSES

Sometimes the lenses of your eyes don't focus correctly. You might have astigmatism, which means the cornea has an irregular shape that causes multiple images or blurry vision. If you are nearsighted, you have myopia. If you are farsighted, you have hyperopia. For each of these vision problems, eye doctors prescribe glasses to help your eyes see things clearly.

REFLECTIONS

Glasses can help our eyes see better. Studying God's Word helps us "see" or understand God better. Make a list of things about God that you would like to understand better.

DON'T STAY IN THE DARKNESS

"I have come as light into the world, so that everyone who believes in me would not remain in darkness."—John 12:46

Many people think everyone is good on the inside even if they make mistakes sometimes. They can't imagine that a "good" person, even if they aren't following Jesus, deserves punishment. They might say, "God would not *actually* send anyone to hell."

At first, their words might sound believable, but their facts are wrong. Jesus addressed this perspective of God when He explained, "The one who rejects me and doesn't receive my sayings has this as his judge: The word I have spoken will judge him on the last day" (John 12:48). In other words, anyone who does not believe in Jesus as Savior has made his or her decision. They have rejected Jesus and the light He brought into the world. This rejection deserves punishment, even if the punishment is as harsh as hell.

The good news is that Jesus also told people how to follow Him so that they could live with Him for eternity: "Everyone who believes in me [will] not remain in darkness" (John 12:46). Jesus explained He did not come to judge the world but to save it! He wants all people to be with Him one day. The most important decision a person ever makes in his or her life is whether to believe Jesus is who He says He is and to follow Him.

PRAY

Ask God to help you trust in Jesus as Savior and Lord of your life.

SEARCHLIGHT VERSES

Read what Jesus told the people in John 12:44–50. Think about what Jesus said, and write your thoughts in the "Reflections" journal on the next page.

BRIGHT IDEA: SUN PRINTS

You'll need dark-colored construction paper (blue, black, purple, etc.), small flat objects (leaves, flowers, small toys, shapes cut from cardboard), clear plastic wrap, and small rocks or other small, heavy weights.

Place the construction paper in direct sunlight. Arrange the small flat items on the paper. Lightly place a piece of plastic wrap over the display to keep things from blowing away. Anchor the plastic with small rocks or other small, heavy items to keep the plastic from blowing away. Wait two to four hours. (The longer you wait, the more vivid the print will be.) Remove the weights and plastic wrap. (Be careful; they could be hot.) Lift each item to see a dark image of the item. The sun faded the paper around each item, revealing its image.

REFLECTIONS

Write your thoughts after reading Jesus's words in the Searchlight Verses (John 12:44–50).

SHINING LIKE THE SUN

While [Peter] was still speaking, suddenly a bright cloud covered them, and a voice from the cloud said, "This is my beloved Son, with whom I am well-pleased. Listen to him!"—Matthew 17:5

Throughout Jesus's ministry, He would sometimes take three disciples—Peter, James, and John—with Him for specific events. We don't know why Jesus chose these three. We do know Peter was chosen as the leader of the early church after Jesus's resurrection; James was the first disciple killed for following Jesus; and John lived to old age and wrote five books we find in our New Testament, including Revelation.

Today's verse is part of a story called the "Transfiguration." Jesus took Peter, James, and John up on a high mountain, where they saw Jesus transfigured—visibly changed—before their eyes. His face shone like the sun and His clothes became as white as light. Moses and Elijah even appeared and talked with Jesus! A bright cloud covered them, and a voice from the cloud said, "This is my beloved Son, with whom I am well-pleased. Listen to him!" Once again, the voice of God made it clear that Jesus was and is His Son!

PRAY

Thank God for the many ways He proved that Jesus is His perfect Son.

SEARCHLIGHT VERSES

Read about the Transfiguration in Matthew 17:1–8.

Bright Idea: Polarized Sunglasses or Eclipse Glasses

Knowing what type of glasses to wear is important. For a normal day in the sun, polarized sunglasses reduce glare by filtering out horizontal light waves. However, if you've ever witnessed a solar eclipse, you had to wear special glasses. Eclipse glasses use specialized filters to protect your eyes. They block almost all visible and invisible (UV and IR) light from the sun. They are the safe choice for looking at the sun during an eclipse.

Reflections

Imagine being on the mountain with Jesus and the three disciples during the Transfiguration. Draw what it might have looked like when Jesus's face shone like the sun, or write about what you might have thought or felt.

GOD'S GLORY

For God who said, "Let light shine out of darkness," has shone in our hearts to give the light of the knowledge of God's glory in the face of Jesus Christ.—2 Corinthians 4:6

After Jesus's resurrection, God chose Paul (also known as Saul) to take the message of the good news about Jesus to people outside of the Jewish nation. Paul traveled to many places and began many churches. He sometimes wrote letters to these churches to remind them about the truth of who Jesus is. The New Testament books of Romans through Philemon are all letters Paul wrote to either churches or individuals.

The letters Paul wrote to the church in the city of Corinth are 1 and 2 Corinthians. In them, he reminded people that God, the Creator of all light, had helped them see and understand that Jesus came for God's glory. Jesus came to be the Savior by taking the punishment for sin and making those who believe in Him right with God. Paul used this reminder to encourage the people in their faith. His words can do the same for us!

PRAY

Ask God to help you have the courage to continue to follow Jesus, no matter what.

SEARCHLIGHT VERSES

Other verses about God's light can encourage us. Read Matthew 4:16. How is this verse encouraging to you? Look back at Isaiah 9:2. How are these two verses similar?

BRIGHT IDEA: MAKE A SUN VISOR

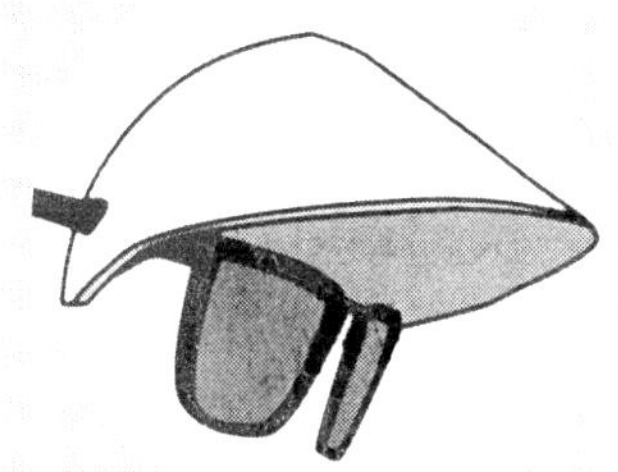

You'll need a cap with a bill, craft foam, pencil, scissors, hole punch, and items to decorate your visor (markers, stickers, etc.).

Use the pencil to trace around the bill of a cap on the craft foam. Cut out the bill shape, and trim the straight edge between the two sides of the bill into a shallow curve that fits your forehead. Punch a hole on both sides of the visor, close to the shallow curve. Decorate your visor. Slip the earpieces of a pair of sunglasses through the holes to add the visor to your sunglasses.

REFLECTIONS

Write a poem praising Jesus for being God's Light to the world, or write out one of the encouraging verses from this devotion.

LUNCHES AND LEFTOVERS

[Jesus] asked Philip, "Where will we buy bread so that these people can eat?" He asked this to test him, for he himself knew what he was going to do.—John 6:5–6

Did you know there were two different occasions when Jesus fed thousands of people with food that would normally only feed a few people? He knew what He was going to do both times. The disciples and the crowds were seeing firsthand evidence of the power of Jesus, the Son of God.

Matthew, Mark, Luke, and John each write about Jesus feeding more than 5,000 people in Galilee. (There were 5,000 men, plus women and children.) A boy shared his small meal of five loaves of bread and two fish. Jesus blessed the food, broke the bread, and told the disciples to serve the crowds. When everyone was full, the disciples went around and gathered twelve baskets of leftovers.

Only Matthew and Mark record the miracle of feeding more than 4,000 people in the Decapolis. This time, the disciples found seven loaves of bread and a few fish. Again, Jesus blessed the food, broke the bread, and told the disciples to share the food with the people. When the crowds were full, the disciples gathered seven baskets of food left over—proof of Jesus's power and His love for people.

PRAY

Jesus had compassion on the people and fed them. Thank Him for the way He loves you and provides for you too.

SEARCHLIGHT VERSES

Read how each Gospel writer describes these two events. Compare and contrast their accounts:

Feeding of the 5,000: Matthew 14:13–21; Mark 6:30–44; Luke 9:10–17; John 6:1–14
Feeding of the 4,000: Matthew 15:32–39; Mark 8:1–10

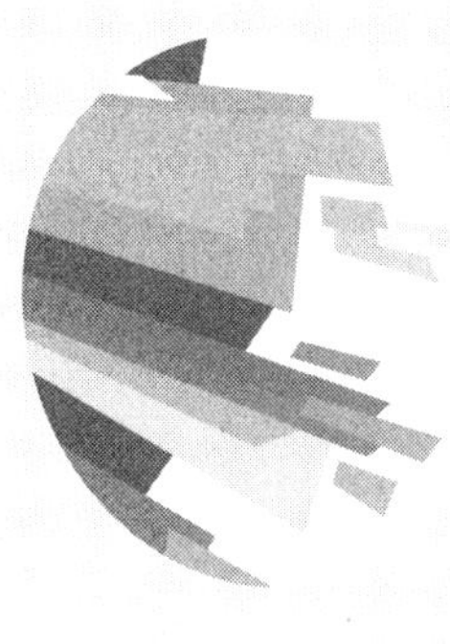

Bright Idea: Seeing the Light

Transparent, *translucent*, and *opaque* are words that describe how light does or does not pass through an object. Clear glass, air, and water are examples of *transparent* things. You can see through them because light passes through them. Frosted glass, wax paper, and many milk jugs are *translucent*. Some light passes through, but the light is scattered. You can't see through them clearly. A brick wall, a tree trunk, or a piece of metal are *opaque*. No light passes through them, so you can't see what is on the other side.

Reflections

Think about how Jesus fed the crowds. Then write or draw pictures of things He provides for you, such as a glass of water, a piece of fruit, or any of your favorite foods.

SO MANY FISH!

When they did this, they caught a great number of fish, and their nets began to tear.—Luke 5:6

The Bible tells of two different miracles when Jesus caused His fishing disciples to have an unbelievable catch. In Luke 5:1–11, Peter and his fellow fishermen were on the lake all night but caught nothing. After Jesus finished teaching the crowd on the lakeshore, He told Peter to try again. Peter didn't see the point, but he obeyed. The catch was amazing! Soon after, Jesus called Peter, Andrew, James, and John to be His disciples.

Later, after Jesus died and rose from the dead, Peter and some of the other disciples were once again fishing and once again had totally empty nets. A man stood on the seashore and called out, asking if they had caught anything. (Peter and the other disciples didn't know the man was Jesus.) The man told them to throw the nets on the right side of the boat. When they obeyed, they caught so many fish that they couldn't pull the heavy nets into the boat! Peter realized the man was Jesus and jumped into the water to swim to shore. Jesus's miracles amazed the disciples back then, and they continue to amaze us today. They shed light on who Jesus really is!

PRAY

Thank Jesus for the many ways He proved He is the powerful Son of God.

SEARCHLIGHT VERSES

Read the full account of both these fishing stories in your Bible. What details stand out to you?

The First Miraculous Catch: Luke 5:1–11
The Second Miraculous Catch: John 21:1–14

BRIGHT IDEA: MAKE A LIGHT TABLE

A light table is a fun way to use diffused light for many great activities. You can buy a light table, or here are three ways to make a simple one:

1. Turn a translucent box (like a food storage box) upside down. Place a light source (flashlight, tap light, or a small string of Christmas lights) underneath.
2. Use a clear under-the-bed storage box with a clear lid. Place a light source inside the box.
3. Use an electronic tablet and choose an all-white screen.

Now find a simple picture (like from a coloring book) and set it on the light table. Then place a white sheet of paper over the picture and trace the image that shows through.

REFLECTIONS

Right before the disciples caught the amazing amounts of fish, they were discouraged. Seeing what Jesus did encouraged them. Write a prayer asking God to help you follow Jesus even when you feel discouraged.

STOPPING THE STORM

[Jesus] got up, rebuked the wind, and said to the sea, "Silence! Be still!" The wind ceased, and there was a great calm.—Mark 4:39

On page 4, we read in John 1:1–3 that Jesus was there in the beginning when all things were created. Because everything was made by Him, He can certainly control all that He has created.

Matthew, Mark, and Luke all include details about what happened one day when Jesus and the disciples crossed the Sea of Galilee by boat. After a long day of teaching, Jesus was tired. He fell asleep in the back of the boat.

Suddenly a fierce storm blew in. The waves were so high that water was coming into the boat! In a panic, the disciples woke Jesus, exclaiming, "Don't you care that we're going to die?" Jesus stood up and spoke to the wind and the waves: "Silence! Be still!" Immediately the wind stopped, and the sea calmed. The disciples were shocked at the power of the Son of God!

When you are in the middle of a storm, it can be hard to remember Jesus is still in control. But He is! No storm—whether in the physical sky or in our personal lives—is too big for Him.

PRAY

It's okay to call out to God when you are afraid or nervous about things like the weather. Thank God for His promise to help you when you are afraid.

SEARCHLIGHT VERSES

Read Matthew 14:22–33 to discover another amazing time Jesus proved His power over storms and the sea.

Bright Idea: Lightning Facts

- Lightning is a bright flash of electricity produced by a thunderstorm.
- The temperature of a lightning bolt is hotter than the sun.
- Count the seconds between when you see a flash of lightning and when you hear thunder. Divide that number by five to determine how many miles away the lightning occurred.
- Lightning can strike up to 25 miles away.
- Lightning sometimes strikes the earth, but most lightning happens between clouds.
- Lightning is dangerous. A good rule to remember is: "When thunder roars, go indoors."

Reflections

Think again about what you read in Matthew 14:22–33. Draw what things might have looked like when Peter tried to walk on the water toward Jesus.

PHYSICAL SIGHT AND SPIRITUAL SIGHT

*"As long as I am in the world,
I am the light of the world."*—John 9:5

While Jesus was on earth, He proved He was the Son of God by doing things only God could do and by honoring God, especially on the Sabbath. John 9 records a great example. (Read the whole chapter to discover everything that happened.) That Sabbath, Jesus and His disciples passed by a man who had been born blind. The disciples thought the man or his parents had sinned and caused the blindness.

Jesus said "no." He explained that the man's blindness allowed God's works to be displayed. After spitting on the ground and making mud, Jesus put the mud on the blind man's eyes and told him to go wash his eyes in the pool of Siloam. The man obeyed, and, for the first time in his life, he could see!

Before healing the blind man, Jesus told His disciples, "I am the light of the world." His light not only can give physical sight, but it also can give spiritual sight. This second kind of sight helps us see the truth about God and our need of a Savior.

PRAY

Sometimes God chooses to heal people who are sick, and sometimes He does not heal them while they are on earth. No matter what, ask God to help you to trust Him and to remember He is powerful over all.

SEARCHLIGHT VERSES

Luke (the writer of the Gospel of Luke) was a doctor. He knew how miraculous Jesus's healings truly were. Look up these stories in Luke's Gospel, and fill in the blank with who was healed and from what disease.

Luke 6:6–11 ____________

Luke 7:1–10 ____________

Luke 13:10–13 ____________

Luke 14:1–6 ____________

BRIGHT IDEA: LIGHT TABLE FUN

On page 31, you learned how to make a light table. Here are a few more light-table activities:

- Create colorful, glowing patterns by setting colorful, flat-bottomed marbles, magnet connection tiles, pieces of cellophane paper, or beads on the table.
- Cover the light table with rice. Use a finger to "draw" in the rice. Smooth it out and start over.

REFLECTIONS

Write about how it feels when you or someone you care about is sick. Then write a prayer asking God to help you remember that He is in control.

LAZARUS, COME OUT!

When Jesus heard it, he said, "This sickness will not end in death but is for the glory of God, so that the Son of God may be glorified through it."—John 11:4

Mary, Martha, and Lazarus were three siblings and Jesus's close friends. John 11 describes a time when Lazarus became very sick. His sisters sent for Jesus, who was teaching on the other side of the Jordan River. When Jesus received their message, He said, "This sickness will not end in death but is for the glory of God." Jesus then waited two days before starting back to Bethany, where His friends lived.

When Jesus arrived, He was told that Lazarus had been dead for four days! But Jesus said this sickness would not end in death—was He wrong? Not at all, because death is not how things ended. Jesus went to the tomb where Lazarus's body was and prayed aloud. He thanked God for always hearing Him. He then prayed, "I know that you always hear me, but because of the crowd standing here I said this, so that they may believe you sent me" (John 11:42). When Jesus called Lazarus to come out of the tomb, he did—Lazarus was alive! God's glory shone brightly that day.

PRAY

Thank God for the many wonderful and amazing things Jesus did to prove He is the Son of God.

SEARCHLIGHT VERSES

Read the full account of Jesus raising Lazarus from the dead in John 11:1–45.

BRIGHT IDEA: COLORFUL FIREWORKS

Do you like big, colorful fireworks shows? The colors come from mineral elements in the fireworks. Bright greens come from barium, and yellows come from sodium. Mixing elements results in more colors: copper produces blues, and strontium produces deep reds, but mixing copper and strontium *together* creates lavender. Gold sparks are produced by iron filings and small pieces of charcoal. Zinc causes smoke effects, and aluminum powder gives fireworks shows their bright flashes and loud BANGs.

REFLECTIONS

Draw a sky filled with your favorite fireworks. Then describe something amazing you know about God.

AUTHORITY OVER HEAVEN AND EARTH

Jesus came near and said to them, "All authority has been given to me in heaven and on earth."—Matthew 28:18

After Jesus rose from the dead, He spent forty days appearing to and talking with His followers. At one point, His disciples traveled to a mountain in Galilee where Jesus gave them some of His final words and instructions before He ascended to heaven. Part of His message was about His power over everything, both while He was still with them and beyond. Jesus said, "All authority has been given to me in heaven and on earth."

Jesus is powerful because He is God and has been given all authority by God. Because of His authority, Jesus could tell His disciples how to continue growing the kingdom of God by making disciples of all nations. Followers of Jesus are to share the good news of salvation; guide people to follow Jesus in obedience, beginning with baptism; and teach all the things Jesus taught.

Jesus included a promise with His command: "And remember, I am with you always, to the end of the age" (Matthew 28:20). Isn't that amazing? And Jesus has the power and authority to keep that promise!

PRAY

Thank Jesus for His promise to be with you always.

SEARCHLIGHT VERSES

The Gospel writers told about many of Jesus's miracles and teachings, which prove He is the Son of God. Read what John wrote in John 21:25, and copy the verse here.

Bright Idea: Fireworks Paintings

Get a black sheet of construction paper, and use one of these ideas to paint a fireworks picture.

- On the end of an empty paper-towel tube, cut 2-inch slits about ¼ of an inch apart. Push down the slitted ends to spread out the strips in a circle. Dip it in paint, then stamp it on your paper.
- Draw firework shapes with a white coloring pencil. Then trace the lines with white school glue and sprinkle regular table salt on the paper. Allow the glue to dry before tapping off the extra salt. Dip a brush in liquid watercolor paint and touch the brush to a line of salt. Watch the color absorb through the salt.
- Dip the tines of a fork into paint and press the back of the fork onto the paper. Repeat in a circular fashion to create a firework.

Reflections

How would you describe God's powerful Son, Jesus, to a friend?

HOSANNA TO THE KING

"Do not be afraid, Daughter Zion. Look, your King is coming, sitting on a donkey's colt."—John 12:15

Not long after Jesus raised Lazarus from the dead, He began His last week of life on earth. As Jesus prepared to enter Jerusalem, He sent two disciples to a nearby village, where He said they would find a donkey and her foal. Jesus told them to bring the donkeys to Him, and if anyone asked what the disciples were doing, they were to say, "The Lord needs them." Everything happened just as Jesus said it would. When the disciples were asked what they were doing with the donkey and her foal, they said the Lord needed them, and the disciples were allowed to go.

The disciples placed some of their clothing on the foal for Jesus to sit on. As He rode the young donkey into Jerusalem, people hurried to greet Him the way they would welcome a king entering a royal city: they spread their coats before Him and covered the road with tree branches.

The crowds shouted "Hosanna!" which means "Save!" or "Save, please." Jesus did come to save, but not in the way the people were expecting. Jesus came not as an earthly king, but as the King of kings—the Savior of the world.

PRAY

Sometimes God doesn't do things the way we expect. Ask God to help you trust Him and remember that His plans are always best.

SEARCHLIGHT VERSES

The event described in today's devotion is often called the Triumphal Entry. It was prophesied in Zechariah 9:9. Compare Zechariah 9:9; Matthew 21:5; and John 12:14–15. What details do all three have in common?

Bright Idea: Fire

Did you know fire is not a "thing"? It's a chemical reaction that releases light and heat. To burn, fire needs fuel, oxygen, and heat. If any one of those three things is removed, the fire stops. Fire can be a good thing when it is safely controlled and used for a purpose, but it can get out of control quickly. It can double in size every thirty to sixty seconds!

Reflections

Bonfires can be a fun time of celebration with your family or at camp. Draw a picture of your favorite things to do around a bonfire.

Betrayed

[Jesus said,] "But all this has happened so that the writings of the prophets would be fulfilled." Then all the disciples deserted him and ran away.—Matthew 26:56

The time had come for Jesus to take on the punishment for all our sins. A lot was about to happen to Jesus, and because He is God, He already knew it all. The prophets had written about it, and Jesus had even warned His disciples. Jesus told His disciples He would be betrayed, arrested, crucified, and die. Jesus also told them He would rise on the third day, which the disciples didn't understand.

Jesus knew one of His twelve chosen disciples, Judas Iscariot, would betray Him. But Jesus continued to treat Judas the same as the other disciples. Judas went to the chief priests and temple police, who offered Judas thirty pieces of silver to betray Jesus. Sadly, Judas agreed.

Matthew tells us that after Jesus was arrested, the other disciples also deserted Him and ran away. Although Jesus knew everything that would happen, He must have been heartbroken to be abandoned by those who should have known and loved Him best.

Pray

Ask God to help you know if your words or actions are hurtful to Him. Ask Him to forgive you and help you make it right.

Searchlight Verses

Peter was a leader in the disciple group, but even Peter had weak moments. Read Luke 22:31–34 and then Luke 22:54–62. How do you think Peter felt?

BRIGHT IDEA: SPINNING COLOR WHEEL

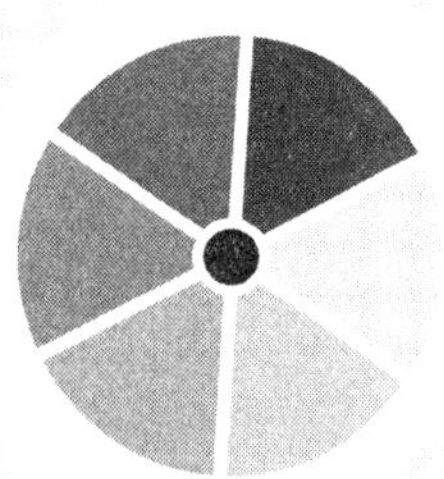

Cut a circle with a five-inch diameter from white poster board or heavy paper. You'll also need markers, about 3 feet of string or yarn, and a sharp pencil.

Mark the center of your circle, and draw lines to create six equal wedges. Color each wedge one of the colors of the rainbow (red, orange, yellow, green, blue, and purple).

Use the pencil to make two small holes in the center of the circle about a half inch apart. Thread the string or yarn through the two holes and tie the ends together.

Slide the circle so it is in the middle of the yarn loop. Hold the ends of the yarn loop and swing the circle to make the yarn twist. After the yarn is tightly twisted, pull the ends and watch the circle spin. What happens to the colors?

REFLECTIONS

Write about a time when you knew the right thing to do, but you had a hard time doing it. What emotions did you feel?

Suffering Servant

But he was pierced because of our rebellion, crushed because of our iniquities; punishment for our peace was on him, and we are healed by his wounds.—Isaiah 53:5

Isaiah 53 is sometimes called the "Suffering Servant" passage because it prophesies many details about Jesus's crucifixion. Even before the difficult night of His arrest, Jesus knew what He would face. He often warned His disciples, even though He knew they would not understand His words until after it was over.

Soon after Peter declared that Jesus was the Son of the living God, Jesus "began to point out to his disciples that it was necessary for him to go to Jerusalem and suffer many things from the elders, chief priests, and scribes, be killed, and be raised the third day" (Matthew 16:21). Several times in the other Gospels, Jesus clearly said He would be arrested, die, and be raised on the third day. Luke 9:45 says His disciples didn't understand because it was hidden from them.

In some ways, the disciples were "in the dark"! God sometimes keeps people from understanding until they are ready to understand or until He is ready for them to know.

Pray

Ask God to help you understand what you can and trust Him with those things you cannot understand.

Searchlight Verses

Read Mark 9:30–32 to discover another time Jesus predicted His death and resurrection. Why do you think the disciples were afraid to ask Jesus what He meant (verse 32)?

BRIGHT IDEA: DARK SKY PLACES

If you live in a city or near a place with lots of ambient light at night, you might think there aren't many stars. To really see planets, stars, and galaxies in the night sky, you need to be in a very dark area. Some places have been labeled as "dark sky" places where there is almost no artificial light—only the night sky. Utah has the highest concentration of dark sky locations in the world!

REFLECTIONS

What do you think about when you look at the stars? Write about how the stars can remind you of Almighty God and His Son, Jesus.

A CHOSEN DEATH

When the centurion . . . saw the way [Jesus] breathed his last, he said, "Truly this man was the Son of God!"—Mark 15:39

Jesus's suffering and crucifixion are hard to read and think about. It's amazing to realize that although He had the power to stop the events of the cross at any time, He didn't. He allowed the suffering and death to happen because they were the only way to take on the punishment for the sin of the world. Because He loved us so much, He endured it all so that we could have forgiveness and a restored relationship with God.

As Jesus hung on the cross, darkness covered the land around noon until about three in the afternoon. When Jesus had done everything He came to do, He said, "It is finished" and breathed His last (John 19:30).

Jesus chose the moment when He would die. A centurion (a Roman soldier) had been keeping watch. When the centurion saw how Jesus breathed His last breath, the soldier said, "Truly this man was the Son of God!"

Jesus chose to endure suffering and to give His life for us. In the darkest of moments, the centurion realized that Jesus is the Son of God. Jesus brought light to the centurion's darkness, and He came to bring light to our darkness too. We only need to trust in Him as our Savior to receive His light.

PRAY

Thank God for Jesus and for all the things Jesus did to make us right with God.

SEARCHLIGHT VERSES

Read Matthew 27:50–54. List some other things that happened the moment Jesus died.

BRIGHT IDEA: CEILING STAR DESIGNS

You'll need a paper cup, either a skewer with a sharp point or a sharpened pencil, a fairly dark room, and a flashlight. Draw a simple design (like a star or cross) on the bottom of the cup. Poke holes about half an inch apart along your design.

Darken the room as much as safely possible. Shine a flashlight into the cup with the bottom of the cup pointed at the ceiling. Do you see your design?

REFLECTIONS

Draw some constellations you've seen in the night sky, then write a prayer to God thanking Him for sending Jesus.

POWERFUL EVIDENCE

He was assigned a grave with the wicked, but he was with a rich man at his death, because he had done no violence and had not spoken deceitfully.—Isaiah 53:9

Detectives compile evidence to shed light on the truth. The more evidence they find, the easier it is to prove the facts—what happened when and who did what.

Thankfully, we don't need detectives to prove that Jesus is God's Son who came to be the Savior of the world. God gave us tons of evidence! Jesus's miracles and the hundreds of people who witnessed them are part of the proof. Jesus also fulfilled hundreds of prophecies about the Savior's birth, life, and death. One of these prophecies is found in Isaiah 53:9. It says the coming Savior would be "with a rich man at his death."

After Jesus died on the cross, Joseph of Arimathea, a rich and important member of the Sanhedrin, offered his own brand-new tomb as Jesus's grave. (In those days, bodies were placed in caves instead of being buried in the ground.) Jesus's body was laid in the tomb, and a heavy stone was rolled across the opening. Joseph didn't know what would happen in just a few days, but he believed Jesus was the proven Son of God, and he wanted to honor Him.

And soon there would be even more powerful evidence of who Jesus is, because He did not stay in that grave!

PRAY

Talk to God about the details He gave the prophets to help us know Jesus is the Son of God. Thank Him for what He is showing you about Jesus.

SEARCHLIGHT VERSES

The chief priests and Pharisees knew Jesus had predicted His resurrection, and they were afraid Jesus's disciples would do something. Read Matthew 27:62–66, and list the precautions the chief priests took to have the tomb securely sealed.

BRIGHT IDEA: SUNRISE, SUNSET

Why is the sky blue during the day and a variety of colors at sunrise and sunset? Sunlight is a mix of colors with each having a different wavelength. Blue and violet have shorter wavelengths and are scattered more easily. That's why daytime skies often look blue. As the sun gets closer to the horizon (at sunrise and sunset), the light must travel through more of the atmosphere. The shorter wavelengths scatter and allow us to see the longer wavelengths of light (red, orange, and yellow).

REFLECTIONS

Use watercolors, pastels, or coloring pencils to draw a beautiful sunrise or sunset. Or write a song to God that praises Him for each new morning.

Come and See!

"He is not here. For he has risen, just as he said. Come and see the place where he lay."—Matthew 28:6

Incredibly, Jesus did not stay in the grave. He arose from the dead! Can you imagine His followers' many emotions when they heard of His resurrection? They likely felt excitement, fear, disbelief, happiness, and even confusion.

Matthew tells about two women who went to the tomb and discovered that an angel had rolled the stone away from the opening. The angel, who resembled a man dressed in gleaming white clothes, said, "He is not here. For he has risen, just as he said." The angel then told them to "come and see" the empty tomb for themselves. The women looked, saw the empty tomb, and were filled with joy. They ran to tell the others about what had happened. They saw the truth that Jesus was alive!

When a light comes on, you can see things that you could not see in the dark. Jesus's disciples were beginning to understand that He had completed the work He had come to do. They saw the evidence, and it was like a bright light turning on. What they couldn't see before they could now see. Just like the angel invited the women to "come and see," Jesus wants us to come, see, and follow Him too.

Pray

Praise God for raising Jesus from the dead. Thank Jesus that He is the proven Son of God who came to defeat sin and death.

Searchlight Verses

Read the four Gospel accounts of the resurrection. Ask God to help you understand the awesomeness of Jesus's resurrection.

Matthew 28:1–10
Mark 16:1–8
Luke 24:1–12
John 20:1–18

BRIGHT IDEA: MARBLED PAPER

You'll need foam shaving cream (not gel), liquid food colors or liquid watercolors, a cookie sheet with edges, a rubber spatula, a plastic knife, a squeegee or piece of cardboard, and plain white paper. Cover your work area with a disposable tablecloth or scrap paper.

Fill the cookie sheet with foam shaving cream. Use the rubber spatula to spread the foam evenly over the whole pan. Squirt several drops of food coloring onto the surface of the shaving cream. Use at least two colors or as many colors as you like. Swirl the colors with the plastic knife.

Place a sheet of paper on top of the shaving cream. Pat gently to be sure all the paper's surface is touching the shaving cream. Remove the paper and lay it flat on a protected surface (your work area with the tablecloth or scrap paper). Use the squeegee or cardboard to carefully scrape off the shaving cream. After your marbled paper is dry, use it to make note cards or wrapping paper, or print a favorite Bible verse on the paper with a permanent marker.

REFLECTIONS

Copy one of your favorite verses about Jesus's resurrection below. Then write about why it is your favorite. (This might be a great verse to copy onto your sheet of marbled paper!)

Repent, and Receive the Gift

"Repent and be baptized, each of you, in the name of Jesus Christ for the forgiveness of your sins, and you will receive the gift of the Holy Spirit."—Acts 2:38

Before Jesus ascended to heaven, He told His disciples the Holy Spirit would soon come and give them the courage and ability to tell others about Jesus. Ten days later the disciples were together when a sound like a rushing wind filled the room. What looked like flames of fire rested on them, and suddenly they were all filled with the Holy Spirit!

Since it was Pentecost, people from many nations, speaking many languages, had come to Jerusalem. Amazingly, the disciples now spoke those languages! When Peter preached, everyone understood his words in their own language. Peter explained who Jesus is, why He came, why He was crucified, and how He had risen from the dead. The people asked, "What should we do?" "Repent and be baptized, each of you, in the name of Jesus Christ for the forgiveness of your sins," Peter said, "and you will receive the gift of the Holy Spirit."

After so much excitement, Peter gave a very simple answer: repent. Once we realize we are sinners, the first thing we need to do is repent, which means to ask forgiveness and turn away from sin. Then we continue to follow Jesus, knowing the Holy Spirit is there to help us.

Pray

If you have never repented of your sins, confess them to God and ask for His forgiveness. If you have repented and trusted in Jesus as your Savior, thank Him for the Holy Spirit, who helps you continue to grow as a Christian.

Searchlight Verses

Some people may not think they have sinned. Others may think they have sinned so badly they can never be forgiven. God has good news for all of us. Read Romans 3:23. Who has sinned? Read Romans 5:8. What has God done for sinners?

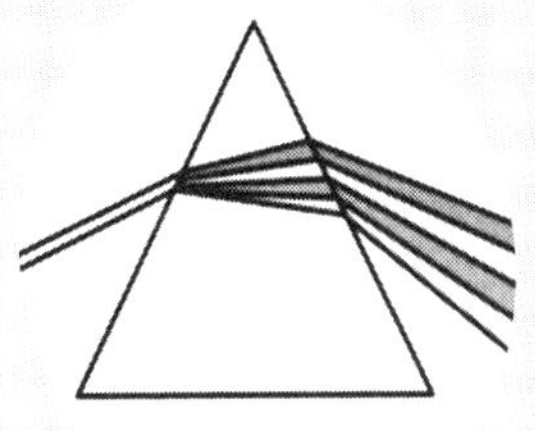

Bright Idea: Reflection or Refraction

A reflection happens when light bounces off a shiny surface back at you so that you see an image. When the shiny surface is smooth, the image is clear (like a mirror or a very still lake). Refraction occurs when the light bends as it passes from one material to another, causing the speed of the light to change. You see refractions when you look at a rainbow or at light through a prism.

Reflections

A reflection in a mirror is not the real person but an image of what the person looks like. When we reflect Jesus to our world it means our words and actions help people around us know more about Him. What are some ways you can reflect Jesus? Write about it here.

Confess, and Bring Sin into the Light

You have set our iniquities before you,
our secret sins in the light of your presence.—Psalm 90:8

Have you ever done something wrong and wished no one would ever find out? Maybe you wished you could forget it too! Psalm 90—known as "a prayer of Moses"—talks about these secret sins. Moses knew that no matter how much we love and follow God, each of us still sins. (*Iniquities* means sins.) His prayer admitted that God is always aware of our sins. Even things we think are hidden in the dark are in the light because of God's presence. That's why confessing (admitting) our sin to God is so important, even after we become a Christian. God gives us amazing promises about how He will forgive us when we confess to Him in repentance and ask for forgiveness.

When we trust in Jesus as our Savior, it doesn't mean we will be perfect and no longer mess up. Christians still sin and need forgiveness to restore their relationship with God. Just like we need to ask our parents or friends to forgive us when we've hurt them, we need to ask God to forgive us. After we become Christians, we are a part of God's family forever, but our sin can strain our relationship with Him. Confessing our sin—bringing our sin into the light—restores our relationship with God.

Pray

Ask God to help you recognize when you have sinned. Talk to God about it and ask Him to forgive you. He will!

Searchlight Verses

Read Romans 10:9–10, 13. What promise is given for those who trust in Jesus as Savior?

Read 1 John 1:9. When Christians confess their sins, what are they promised?

BRIGHT IDEA: MIRROR PORTRAITS

Try one of these fun mirror activities:

- Stand in front of a mirror. Use a dry erase marker to trace your face. Step back and see how you did.
- Hold a clear disposable plate in front of your face. Ask a friend to use a dry erase marker to trace your face. Use another clear disposable plate to trace your friend's face.

REFLECTIONS

Write a prayer to God, thanking Him for His promise of forgiveness. If your sinful choices are coming to mind, write a prayer confessing them to God.

Believe, and Share the Light

"You are the light of the world. A city situated on a hill cannot be hidden."—Matthew 5:14

It's not fun to be left out, to not make a team, or to not be invited to a party. But the book of Acts reminds us that all of us are invited to follow Jesus. Anyone who believes in Him will be saved.

In Acts 10, God helped Peter understand that the Good News about Jesus was for everyone in the world, regardless of where they lived or who they were. In that same story, a Roman centurion named Cornelius gathered his friends and family together so that they could hear about Jesus. Cornelius's family heard about Jesus and believed in Him.

Everyone who believes in Jesus and trusts in Him for salvation becomes a part of God's forever family! When we share His Good News with others, we are sharing the true Light with the world. We get to help others learn about Jesus and invite them to trust in Him as Savior.

Pray

Thank God that the Good News about Jesus is for everyone who believes in Jesus as Savior.

Searchlight Verses

The story of Peter and Cornelius is a great one to read. You can find it in Acts 10:1–48.

BRIGHT IDEA: ABSORPTION

Reflection is when light bounces back, like when you see an image in a mirror or when you see colors, such as the green of a leaf. Refraction is when light bends as it moves through various elements, like water or air. But light can also be *absorbed*. When light is absorbed, it turns into another kind of energy, such as heat. When you wear dark clothes on a sunny day, the light is absorbed and transformed into heat, making you feel hotter.

REFLECTIONS

Think about how Jesus's love reaches people all over the world. Draw a globe or make a list of as many countries as you can think of. Imagine people in all these places, far and wide, believing in Jesus!

TRUST, AND REFLECT JESUS

But I trust in you, LORD; I say, "You are my God."—Psalm 31:14

Each day, we decide where we put our trust. Will we trust in ourselves and listen to the lies of the world? Or will we trust in Jesus, who always leads us toward God?

In Luke 18, Jesus was speaking to some people who trusted in themselves and their own good deeds to make their lives right with God. They often looked down on people they thought were not as good as they were.

Jesus told a parable about two different men at the temple: a Pharisee (a temple leader) and a tax collector (a person almost everyone hated). The Pharisee prayed loudly about the great things he did and how he kept all the temple rules. He even thanked God that he wasn't like the tax collector. Meanwhile, the tax collector stood near the back of the temple and wouldn't even look up. In repentance he said, "God, have mercy on me, a sinner!"

Jesus's parable means that instead of bragging about ourselves, God wants us to stay humble and put our trust in Him. When we humbly reflect Jesus by trusting Him and following His commands, we share His light with others.

PRAY

Ask God to help you trust in Him, not yourself, and live in ways that honor Him.

SEARCHLIGHT VERSES

Read Jesus's parable about the Pharisee and the tax collector in Luke 18:9–14.

Bright Idea: Refraction Experiments

Try a couple of refraction experiments. Remember that refraction is when light moves through something that causes the speed to change and the light to bend.

- You need a clear glass or jar with straight sides. Fill it a little more than halfway with water. Place a pencil or straw in the water and look at it from the side. Does it look like the pencil or straw is broken? That's refraction!
- Draw an arrow pointing to the right on an index card or small piece of paper. Look through a clear glass or jar with straight sides while you move the picture of the arrow behind the glass. Did it flip?

Reflections

Write about ways you can reflect (imitate) Jesus and be a light to those around you.

THE COURAGE TO OBEY

The LORD is my light and my salvation—whom should I fear? The LORD is the stronghold of my life—whom should I dread?—Psalm 27:1

Life was not easy for the disciples and the other believers of the early church. They were often arrested and put in prison for preaching about Jesus and obeying His command to go and tell others about Him. But the Holy Spirit gave the disciples courage and words to say.

One time, the high priest and the Sadducees were so jealous that they had some of the disciples arrested and put into the public jail. During the night, an angel of the Lord opened the prison doors and let them out. The angel told them to return to the temple and tell the people about Jesus and how to follow Him (Acts 5:17–21).

Later, when the high priest and the Sanhedrin (the combined group of Sadducees and Pharisees) sent for the disciples, the jail was empty even though it was still locked! They found the disciples teaching in the temple and ordered them to stop teaching in the name of Jesus. Peter and the other disciples said, "We must obey God rather than people" (Acts 5:22–32).

Just like the early church, we need courage to obey God and tell others about Jesus. Thankfully, we have the same Helper as the disciples! The Holy Spirit will help us know when to speak and what to say.

PRAY

Ask God to help you to trust the Holy Spirit, to have courage to obey Him, and to tell others about Jesus.

SEARCHLIGHT VERSES

Read about the disciples' experience in Acts 5:17–42. Write down some amazing facts from this story.

BRIGHT IDEA: WHAT MAKES A RAINBOW?

God gave the first rainbow as a reminder of His promise to never again destroy the entire earth with a flood. Rainbows are beautiful and remind us of God's promise.

But how does a rainbow happen? When sunlight interacts with water droplets, a refraction and a reflection of light occurs. Sunlight (which contains all colors) enters the water droplet and is bent (refracted). The light is reflected off the back of the water droplet and refracted again as it exits the water droplet. All of that bouncing and bending of light separates the white light into individual colors.

REFLECTIONS

Draw a picture of a rainbow, and list some of God's promises under your picture.

FOLLOWING THE LIGHT

Your word is a lamp for my feet and a light on my path.—Psalm 119:105

We all have days when life seems dark or when we need direction during hard times. In those times (and at all times), we can remember two things: God created light, and God gave His Son, Jesus, to be the Light of the world.

That means we always have God's light to guide our way! When we trust in Jesus as our Savior, He gives us the Holy Spirit to help us, and He has given us His Word—the Bible—to be a lamp for our feet and a light on our path.

God provides all we need when we need it through the Holy Spirit and the Bible. We can reflect God's love and care by sharing His light with the world and telling others about Him.

The best news is that God's plans and promises are not only for here and now, but also for eternity! We find a wonderful promise in Revelation 22:5: "Night will be no more; people will not need the light of a lamp or the light of the sun, because the Lord God will give them light, and they will reign forever and ever."

The most important thing we will ever do is trust Jesus as our Savior. Then, as we study the Bible, pray, and learn from other Christians, we grow in knowledge and in our relationship with Jesus. When we follow Him, we have the only true Light we need!

PRAY

Thank God for the way He has provided for your past, present, and future.

SEARCHLIGHT VERSES

Read John 8:12 again, and copy it here. Memorize it if you haven't already.

BRIGHT IDEA: MAKE A RAINBOW

- Place a mirror in a bowl of water. Prop the mirror so that it sits at an angle. Shine a flashlight (the flashlight on a phone works) on the mirror and look on the wall or ceiling for a rainbow. You can also hold a white piece of paper above the bowl to "catch" the rainbow. If you don't see a rainbow immediately, you may need to move to a darker room. The "rainbow" will be along the edge of the circle of light.
- Shine a flashlight on the shiny side of a CD and look around for the rainbow. Move the rainbow (or rainbows!) by moving the CD.

REFLECTIONS

Write a prayer to God thanking Him for all the ways He has proven His love for you by sending His Son, Jesus.

Illumination Station Devotional *is lovingly dedicated to the amazing VBS publishing team at Lifeway. These precious friends pour their hearts and prayers into making Vacation Bible School resources that shine the light on who Jesus is to people around the world.*

–Rhonda